This **Picture Mammoth** *belongs to*

_____

_____

Catherine and Laurence Anholt

ONE, TWO, THREE,
COUNT WITH
ME

One, two, three,
Count with me,
Counting everything we see.

2 eyes

1 nose

10 fingers

1 tummy

2 legs

10 toes

Let's count together.

Can you count from one to ten
Round the park and back again ?

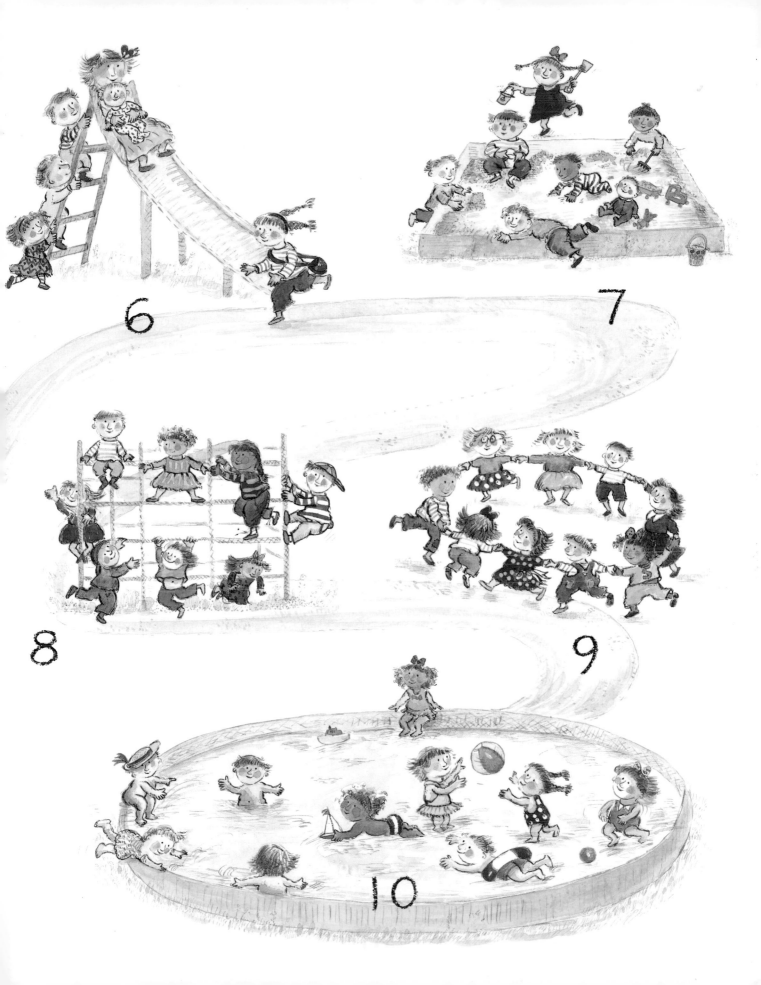

6

7

8

9

10

Count with me in the garden...

How many flowers?

How many bees?

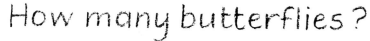

How many butterflies?

How many trees?

How many clothes are hanging out to dry ?

How many kites are flying in the sky ?

counting bikes,

counting cars,

counting trains,

counting lorries,

counting boats,

counting planes.

We can count animals ...

1 mouse in a house,

2 bears on a chair,

3 goats in a boat,

4 foxes in boxes,

5 kittens in mittens,

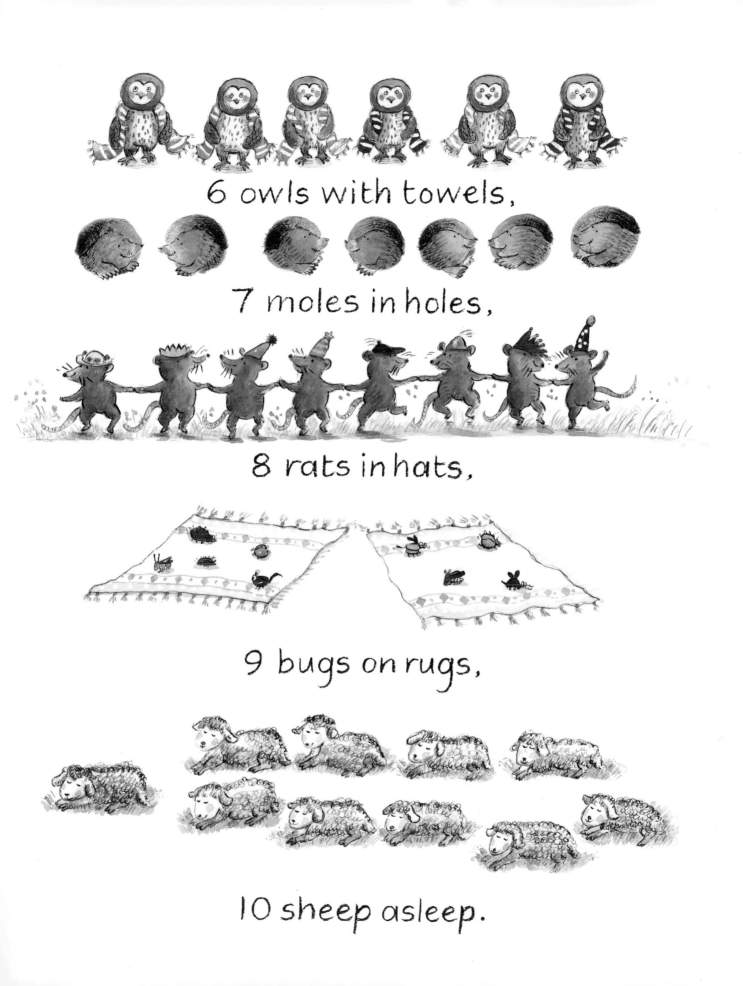

6 owls with towels,

7 moles in holes,

8 rats in hats,

9 bugs on rugs,

10 sheep asleep.

The farmer says it isn't hard
To count the animals in the yard –
How many chickens pecking on the path?
How many ducklings going for their bath?
How many cows are waiting to be fed?
How many piglets are hiding in the shed?

I like counting every day,
Let's count the children as they play.

Monday

Tuesday

Wednesday

Thursday

Friday

Saturday

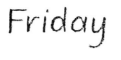

Sunday

How many days in the week?

We can count BIG things...

and LITTLE things too...

birds

bricks

bubbles

beads

stones

shells

stamps

seeds

raisins

ribbons

rings

rice

money

marbles

moths

mice

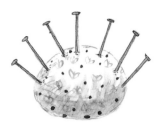   

pins   pens   paints   peas

fruit   freckles   flowers   fleas

badges   bells   bears   bags

fish   flies   fairies   flags

Counting colours is fun ...

One white clown
all by herself,

Two brown bears
on a purple shelf,

Three green frogs on an orange bed,

Four big lorries painted red,

Five black spiders, six pink balloons,

Seven yellow teacups with seven yellow spoons,

Eight blue dolls and nine gold rings,

Ten is a box full of colourful things.

Now we can count anything!

10 big shoes for 10 big feet,

20 puppies, aren't they sweet!

100 lovely things to eat, and . . .

a million stars above my street.

First published in Great Britain 1994
by William Heinemann Ltd
Published 1995 by Mammoth
an imprint of Reed Consumer Books Ltd
Michelin House, 81 Fulham Road, London SW3 6RB
and Auckland, Melbourne, Singapore and Toronto

Copyright © Catherine and Laurence Anholt 1994

Reprinted 1995, 1997

ISBN 0 7497 1923 0

A CIP catalogue record for this title
is available from the British Library

Produced by Mandarin Book Production
Printed and bound in Hong Kong